Oceans of the World
The Southern Ocean

By Lauren Gordon

Table of Contents

The Southern Ocean	3
Words to Know	22
Index	23
Comprehension Questions	23
About the Author	24

A Starfish Book

Teaching Tips for Caregivers:

As a caregiver, you can help your child succeed in school by giving them a strong foundation in language and literacy skills and a desire to learn to read.

This book helps children grow by letting them practice reading skills.

Reading for pleasure and interest will help your child to develop reading skills and will give your child the opportunity to practice these skills in meaningful ways.

- Encourage your child to read on her own at home
- Encourage your child to practice reading aloud
- Encourage activities that require reading
- Establish a reading time
- Talk with your child
- Give your child writing materials

Teaching Tips for Teachers:

Research shows that one of the best ways for students to learn a new topic is to read about it.

Before Reading

- Read the "Words to Know" and discuss the meaning of each word.
- Read the back cover to see what the book is about.

During Reading

- When a student gets to a word that is unknown, ask them to look at the rest of the sentence to find clues to help with the meaning of the unknown word.
- Ask the student to write down any pages of the book that were confusing to them.

After Reading

- Discuss the main idea of the book.
- Ask students to give one detail that they learned in the book by showing a text dependent answer from the book.

The Southern Ocean

There are five oceans on Earth.
One is the Southern Ocean.

The continent of Antarctica is at Earth's **South Pole**.

The Southern Ocean surrounds Antarctica.

It is sometimes called the Antarctic Ocean.

The Southern Ocean is the second smallest ocean in the world.

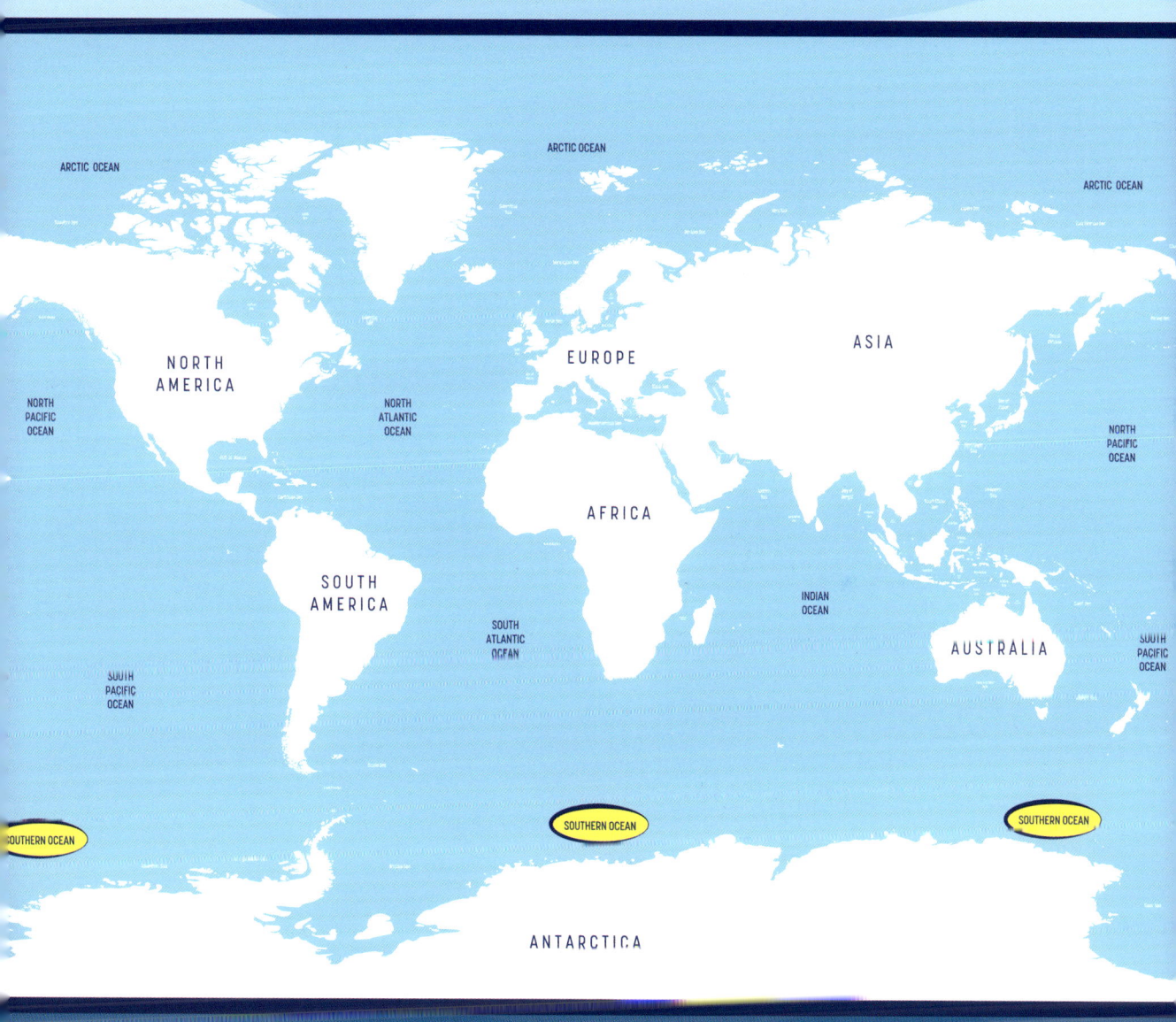

The Southern Ocean is the newest ocean to be **recognized**.

In honor of World Oceans Day 2021, National Geographic declared the Southern Ocean as the fifth ocean on Earth.

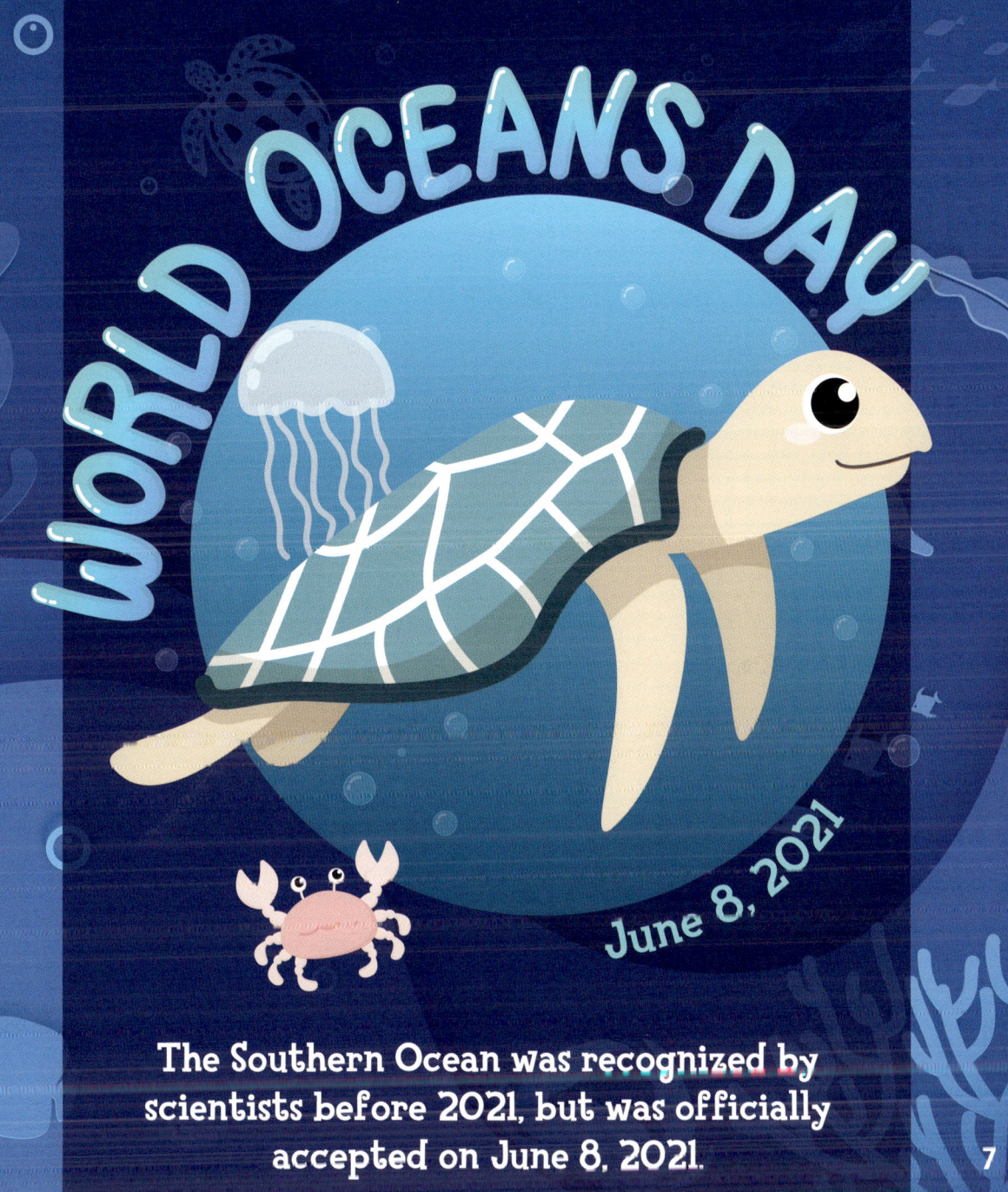

The Southern Ocean was recognized by scientists before 2021, but was officially accepted on June 8, 2021.

Brr! The water is cold!

The temperature of the Southern Ocean ranges from 28 to 50 degrees Fahrenheit (-2 to 10 degrees Celsius).

The Southern Ocean is the only ocean that goes all the way around the globe!

The Southern Ocean has some of the strongest winds on Earth!

Intense winds, powerful **currents**, and tall waves can cause storms.

The Southern Ocean has an average depth of over 10,000 feet (3,000 meters).

At its deepest, the Southern Ocean can be over 24,000 feet (7,000 meters) deep.

Emperor penguins can be four feet (one meter) tall and weigh up to 99 pounds (45 kilograms).

Many animals live in and near the Southern Ocean.

The world's largest penguin, the emperor penguin, lives in Antarctica.

The water in the Southern Ocean has lots of **nutrients**.

This encourages **plankton** to grow.

Plankton is an important source of food for fish, mammals, and birds.

Krill are tiny, shrimp-like **crustaceans**.

Krill eat plankton.

Seals and many other animals eat krill to survive.

Huge swarms of krill can float in the ocean.

The Southern Ocean is in danger.

The water is getting warmer, causing plankton and krill to die.

Without these food sources, many animals will not survive.

Words to Know

crustaceans (kruh-STAY-shuhnz): sea creatures with a hard outer skeleton, such as crabs, lobsters, or shrimp

currents (KUR-uhnts): movements of water in a definite direction in an ocean or river

nutrients (NOO-tree-uhnts): substances in food, such as proteins and vitamins, that help people, animals, and plants live and grow

plankton (PLANGK-tuhn): a mixture of very small plants and animals floating in water

recognized (REK-uhg-nized): identified, appreciated, or acknowledged someone or something

South Pole (south pohl): the most southern part of Earth located at the bottom tip of Earth's axis

Index

Antarctica 3, 4, 5, 9, 14
depth 12
emperor penguin 14
plankton 16, 18, 20

storms 10
temperature 8
winds 10
World Oceans Day 6, 7

Comprehension Questions

1. True or False: The Northern Ocean is one of five oceans in the world.
2. True or False: The Southern Ocean is sometimes called the Australian Ocean.
3. True or False: Penguins, seals, and krill are some of the animals that live in the Southern Ocean.
4. True or False: The Southern Ocean was recognized as an ocean in 2021.
5. True or False: The Southern Ocean is the only ocean that goes all the way around Earth.

Answers
1. False 2. False 3. True 4. True 5. True

About the Author

Lauren Gordon is originally from New York and now lives in Florida. She lives with her husband and two children. In her free time, she likes to read and spend time with her family.

Written by: Lauren Gordon
Design by: Jen Bowers
Editor: Kim Thompson

Photographs from Shutterstock.com: Cover image ©2018 David Herraez Calzada, backgound ©2012 Andrey_Kuzmin, water globe ©2012 zffoto; p.2 and throughout backgroud ©elic; p.3 and throughout background ©Aleksandra Bataeva, globes ©Designua; p.5 ©Pyty; p.7 ©asiandelight; p.9 ©ugljesa; p.11 ©2020 RugliG; p.13 ©2014 RyanMinus; p.15 ©2009 TravelMediaProductions; p.17 magnifying glass ©Pavlo S, background ©2015 borzywoj, ©2019 Choksawatdikorn; p.18 ©BlueRingMedia; p.19 © 2019 Apple Pho; p.21 ©2019 ENVIROSENSE

Library of Congress PCN Data
Oceans of the World / Gordon
The Southern Ocean
ISBN 978-1-63897-451-2 (hard cover)
ISBN 978-1-63897-566-3 (paperback)
ISBN 978-1-63897-681-3 (EPUB)
ISBN 978-1-63897-796-4 (eBook)
Library of Congress Control Number: 2021953363

Printed in the United States of America.

Seahorse Publishing Company
www.seahorsepub.com

Copyright © 2023 **SEAHORSE PUBLISHING COMPANY**

All rights reserved. No part of this publication may be reproduced, stored in a retrieval system or be transmitted in any form or by any means, electronic, mechanical, photocopying, recording, or otherwise, without the prior written permission of Seahorse Publishing Company.

Published in the United States
Seahorse Publishing
PO Box 771325
Coral Springs, FL 33077